51 MUST-HAVE MODERN WORSHIP HITS

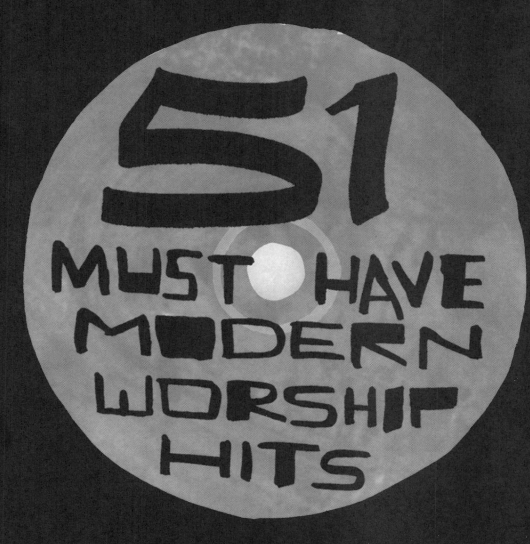

ISBN-13: 978-1-4234-3077-3
ISBN-10: 1-4234-3077-8

HAL•LEONARD® CORPORATION

7777 W. BLUEMOUND RD. P.O. BOX 13819 MILWAUKEE, WI 53213

Visit Hal Leonard Online at
www.halleonard.com

CONTENTS

ALL THE EARTH WILL SING YOUR PRAISES

Words and Music by
PAUL BALOCHE

And all the earth will sing Your prais - es.

You lived, You died,

You said in three days You would rise; ___ You did.

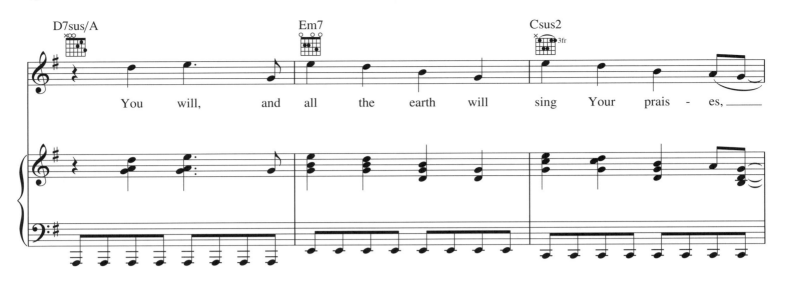

You will, and all the earth will sing Your prais - es, _____

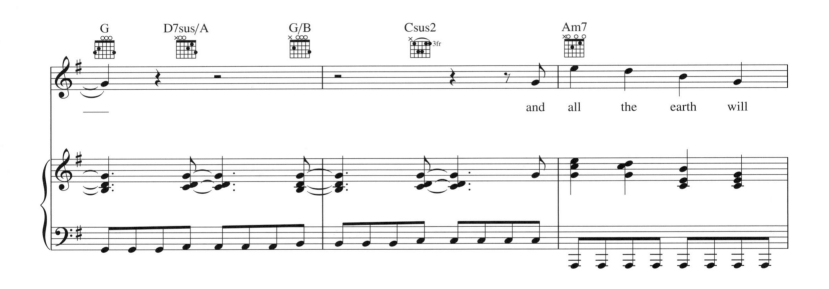

_____ and all the earth will

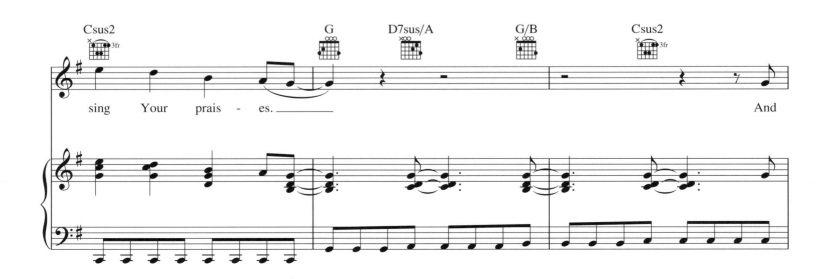

sing Your prais - es. _____ And

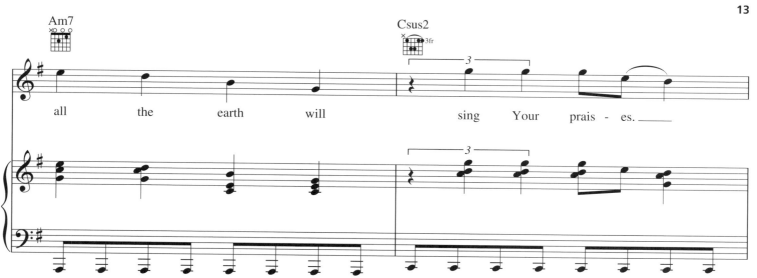

all the earth will sing Your prais - es. _____

And

all the earth will sing Your prais - es, _____

rit.

AMAZED

Words and Music by
JARED ANDERSON

BETTER IS ONE DAY

Words and Music by
MATT REDMAN

Driving

How love - ly is Your dwell - ing place,

O Lord _ Al - might - y. My soul longs and

e - ven faints for You. For

BLESSED BE YOUR NAME

Words and Music by MATT REDMAN
and BETH REDMAN

*Recorded a half step lower.

EVERYDAY

Words and Music by
JOEL HOUSTON

With energy

What to say?__ Lord, it's You who gave__ me life,__ and I__

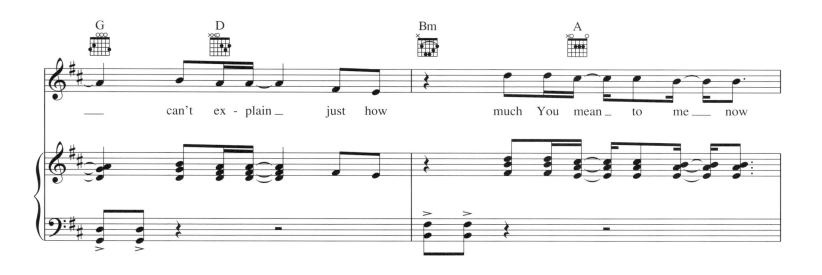

__ can't ex-plain__ just how much You mean__ to me__ now

that You have saved__ me, Lord. I give all that__ I am__ to You,__

COME, NOW IS THE TIME TO WORSHIP

Words and Music by
BRIAN DOERKSEN

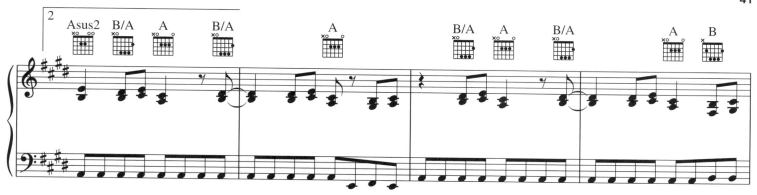

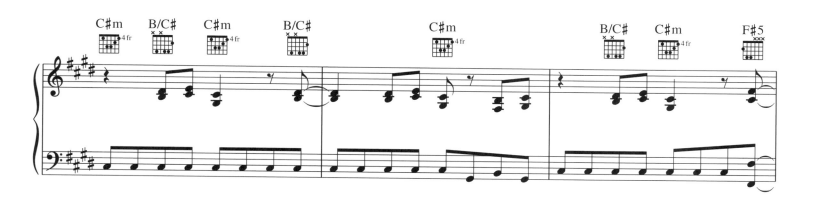

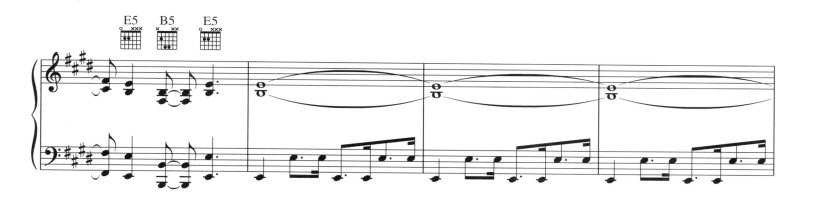

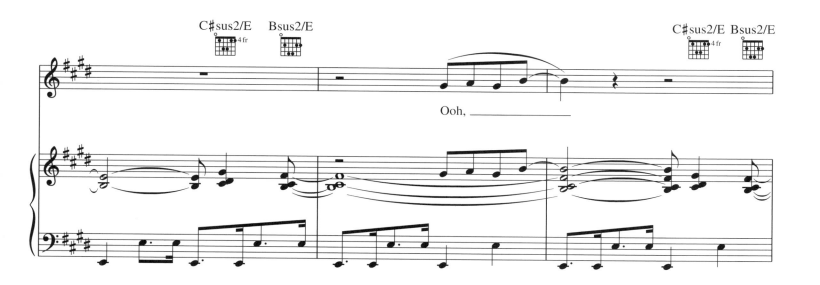

Ooh, _____

EVERY MOVE I MAKE

Words and Music by
DAVID RUIS

FILLED WITH GLORY

Words and Music by MICHAEL GUNGOR
and LISA GUNGOR

FOREVER

Words and Music by
CHRIS TOMLIN

FRIEND OF GOD

Words and Music by MICHAEL GUNGOR
and ISRAEL HOUGHTON

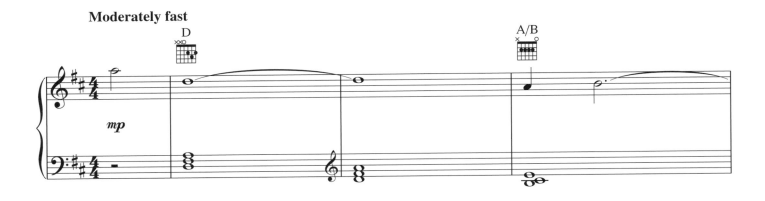

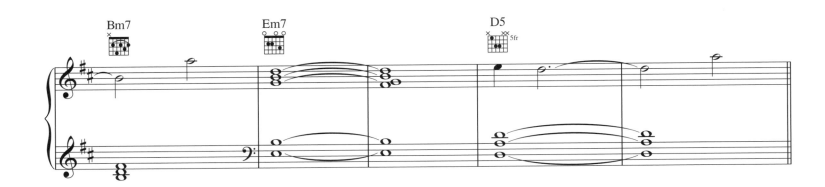

Who am I ___ that You ___ are mind-ful ___ of ___ me,

HALLELUJAH
(Your Love Is Amazing)

Words and Music by BRENTON BROWN
and BRIAN DOERKSEN

(1., 3.) Your love is __ a-maz - ing, stead-y and un-chang - ing. Your love is __ a moun-
(2.) -ing, I can feel __ it ris - ing, all the joy __ that's grow-

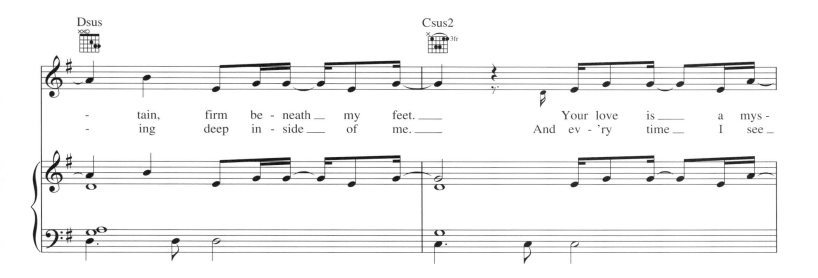

-tain, firm be-neath __ my feet. __ Your love is __ a mys-
-ing deep in-side __ of me. __ And ev-'ry time __ I see __

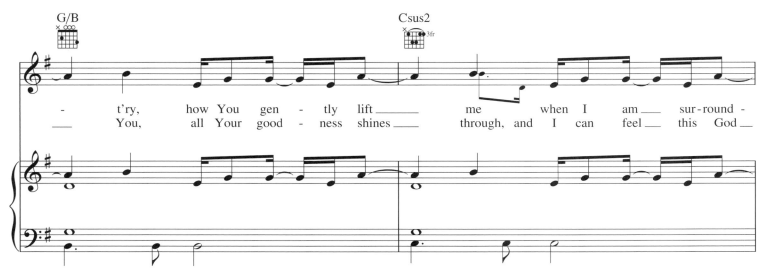

-t'ry, how You gen - tly lift _____ me when I am __ sur-round-
___ You, all Your good - ness shines ____ through, and I can feel __ this God __

GOD IS GREAT

Words and Music by
MARTY SAMPSON

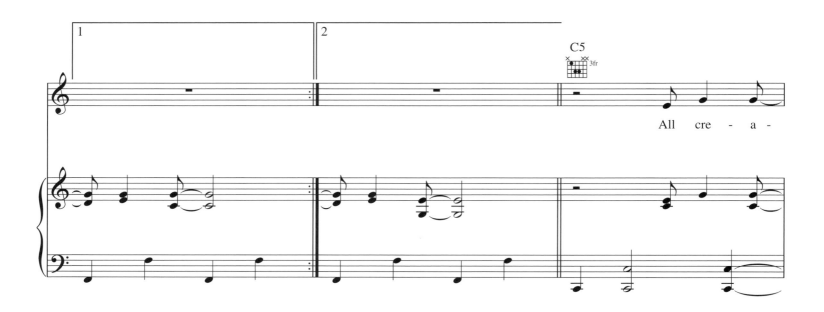

All cre - a -

-tion cries ___ to You,

GOD OF WONDERS

Words and Music by MARC BYRD
and STEVE HINDALONG

Lord of all ___ cre - a - tion, ___
Ear - ly in ___ the morn - ing ___

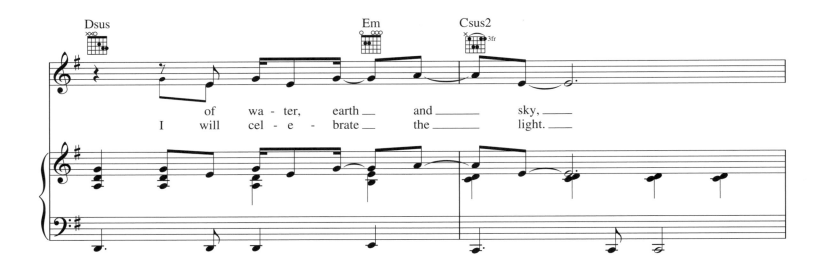

of wa - ter, earth ___ and ___ sky, ___
I will cel - e - brate ___ the ___ light. ___

the heav - ens are Your tab - er - na - cle; ___
And as I stum - ble in the dark - ness, ___

HE REIGNS

Words and Music by PETER FURLER
and STEVE TAYLOR

THE HEART OF WORSHIP

Words and Music by
MATT REDMAN

HERE I AM TO WORSHIP

Words and Music by
TIM HUGHES

- er know _ how much _ it cost _ to see _ my sin _ up - on _

_ that cross. _ And I'll nev - _ that cross. _ Here I am to

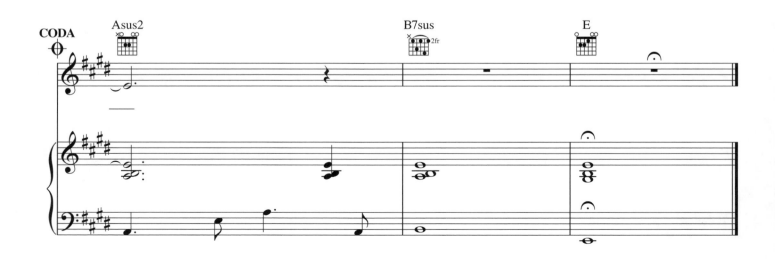

I COULD SING OF YOUR LOVE FOREVER

Words and Music by
MARTIN SMITH

HOLY AND ANOINTED ONE

Words and Music by
JOHN BARNETT

HOSANNA
(Praise Is Rising)

Words and Music by PAUL BALOCHE
and BRENTON BROWN

With a driving beat

Praise _____ is
Hear _____ the

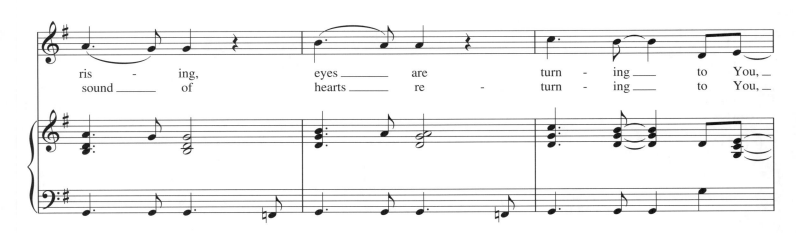

ris - ing,   eyes _____ are   turn - ing _____ to You, _____
sound _____ of   hearts _____ re - turn - ing _____ to You, _____

116

HOW GREAT IS OUR GOD

Words and Music by CHRIS TOMLIN,
JESSE REEVES and ED CASH

* Recorded a half step lower.

I AM FREE

Words and Music by
JON EGAN

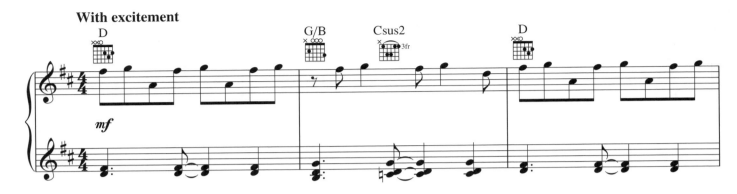

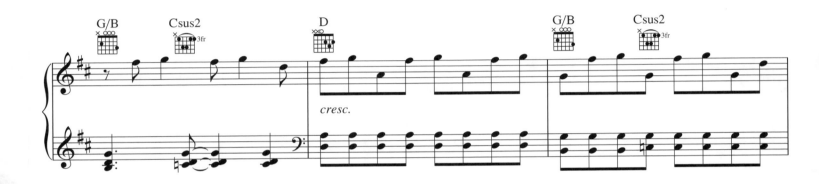

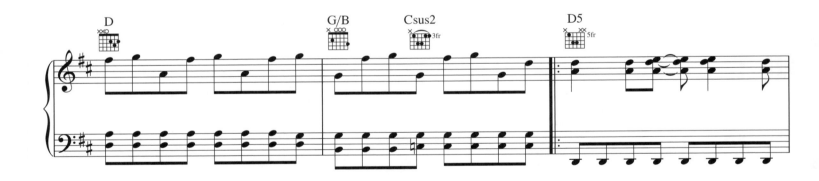

Lead vocal ad lib. on repeat

Through You __ the blind __ will see, __

through You __ the mute __ will sing, __ through You __ the dead __

__ will rise, __ through You __ our hearts __ will praise, __

through You ____ the dark - ness flees, __

Oh, _____ oh, _____ oh, _____

I GIVE YOU MY HEART

Words and Music by
REUBEN MORGAN

I WILL BOAST

Words and Music by
PAUL BALOCHE

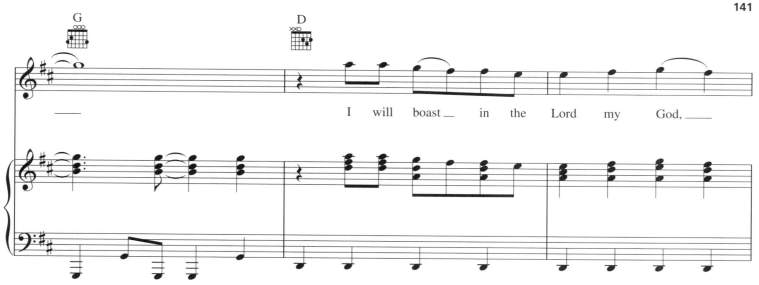

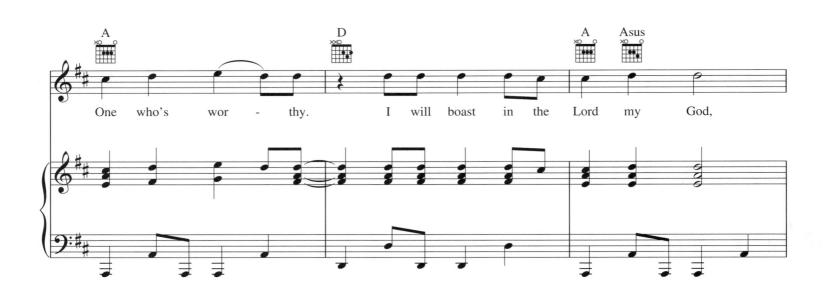

LOVE SONG

Words and Music by
JASON MORANT

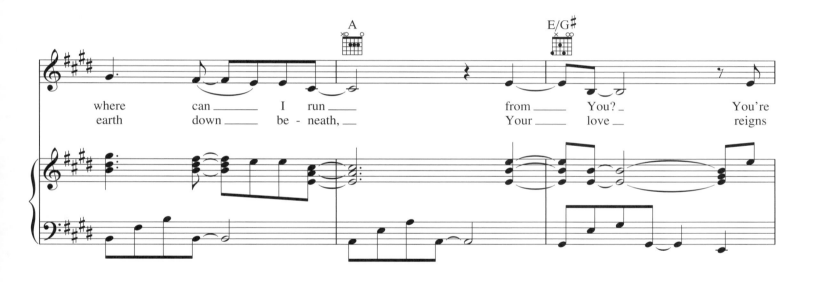

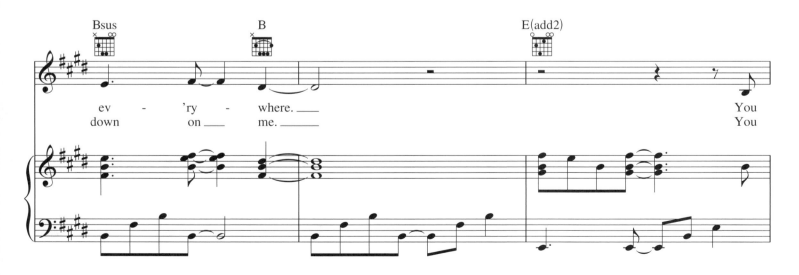

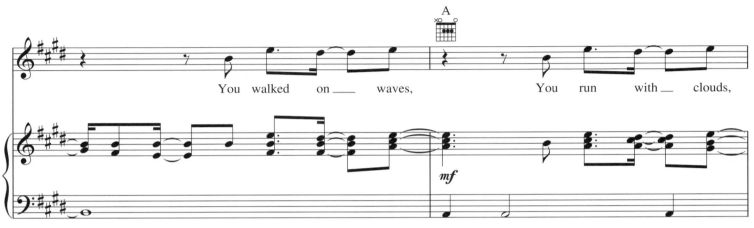

INDESCRIBABLE

Words and Music by LAURA STORY
and JESSE REEVES

Recorded a half step higher.

JESUS, LOVER OF MY SOUL

Words and Music by JOHN EZZY,
DANIEL GRUL and STEPHEN McPHERSON

LET THE PRAISES RING

Words and Music by
LINCOLN BREWSTER

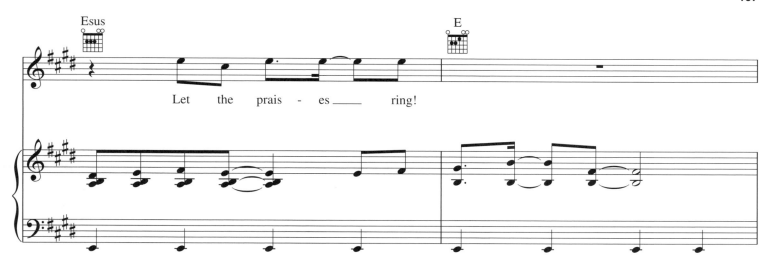

Let the prais - es ___ ring!

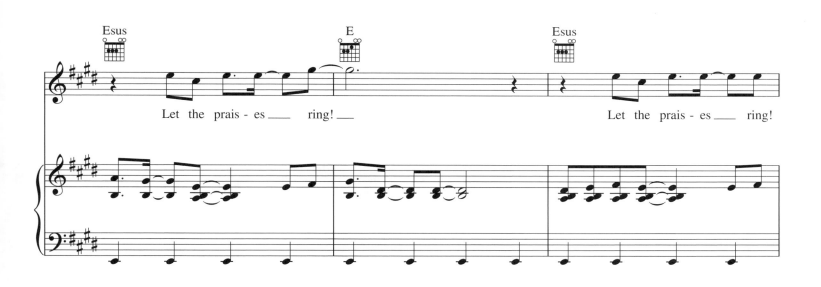

Let the prais - es ___ ring! ___   Let the prais - es ___ ring!

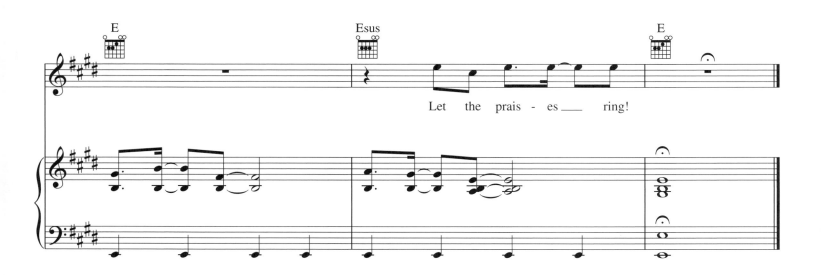

Let the prais - es ___ ring!

LOVE THE LORD

Words and Music by
LINCOLN BREWSTER

Da da dum   da da dum da da da. ___ Da da dum   oh, ___ yeah. ___

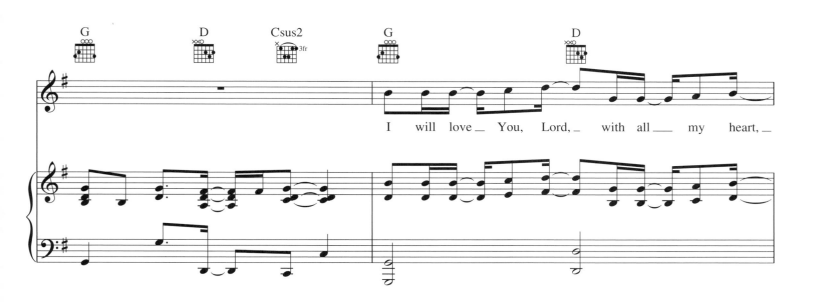

I will love ___ You, Lord, ___ with all ___ my   heart, ___

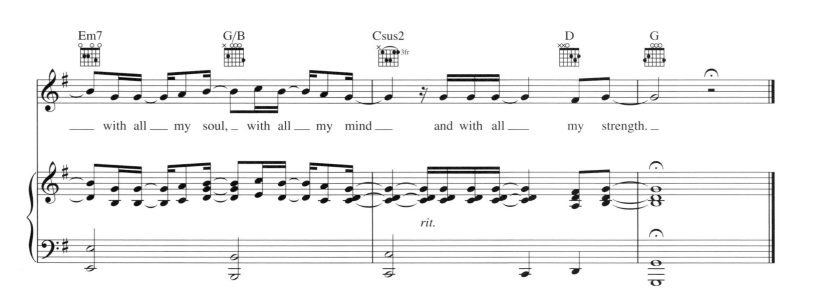

___ with all ___ my soul, ___ with all ___ my mind ___   and with all ___   my   strength. ___

MAJESTY
(Here I Am)

Words and Music by MARTIN SMITH
and STUART GARRARD

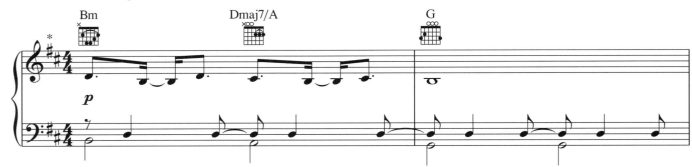

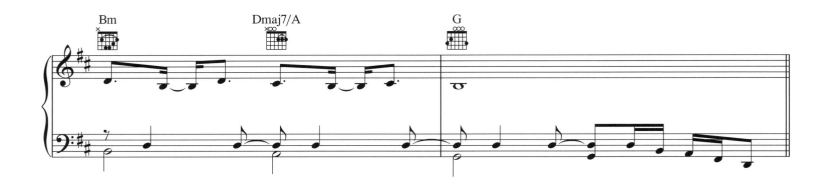

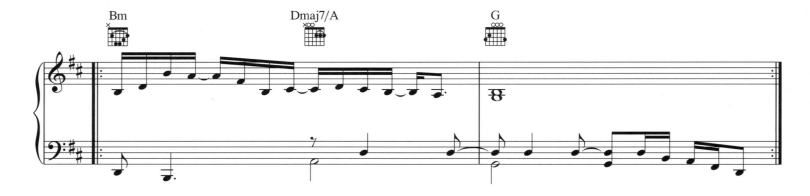

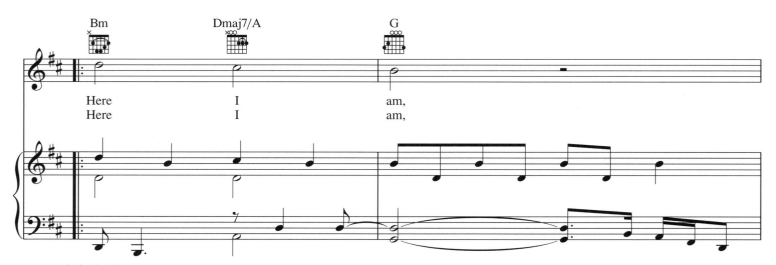

Here   I   am,
Here   I   am,

*Recorded a half step lower.

MY REDEEMER LIVES

Words and Music by
REUBEN MORGAN

MORE LOVE, MORE POWER

Words and Music by
JUDE DEL HIERRO

NOT TO US

Words and Music by CHRIS TOMLIN
and JESSE REEVES

Recorded a half step lower.

OFFERING

Words and Music by
PAUL BALOCHE

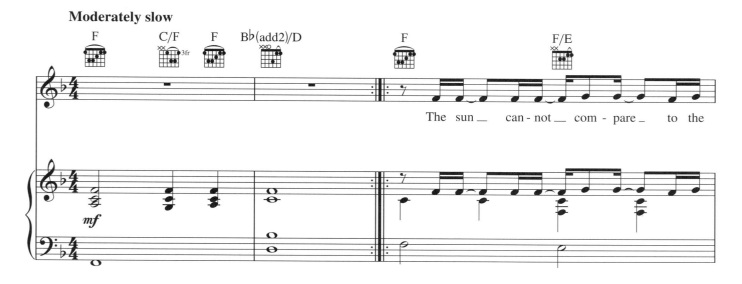

The sun _ can - not _ com - pare _ to the

glo - ry of _ Your love. _ There is _ no shad - ow in _ Your pres -

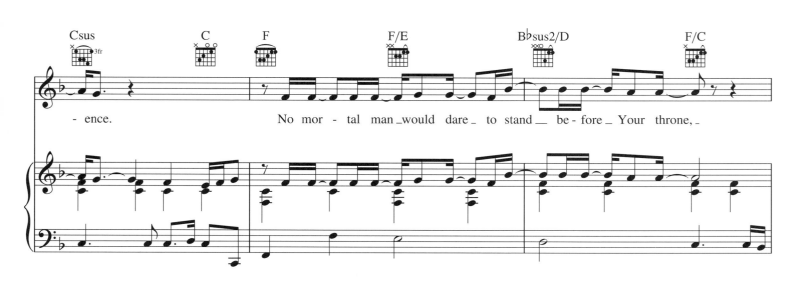

- ence. No mor - tal man _ would dare _ to stand _ be - fore _ Your throne, _

NOW THAT YOU'RE NEAR

Words and Music by
MARTY SAMPSON

OPEN THE EYES OF MY HEART

Words and Music by
PAUL BALOCHE

RESCUE

Words and Music by
JARED ANDERSON

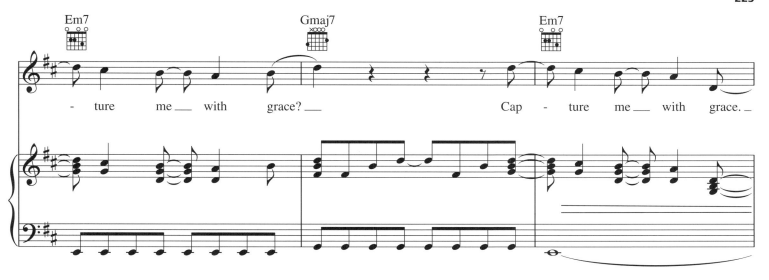

-ture me ___ with grace? ___ Cap - ture me ___ with grace. ___

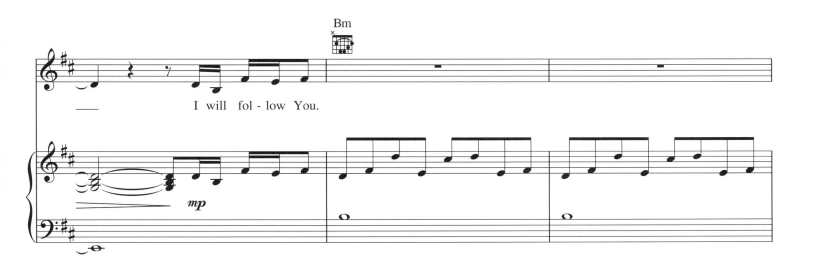

___ I will fol - low You.

This world has noth - ing for me.

SING FOR JOY

Words and Music by
LAMONT HIEBERT

TODAY
(As for Me and My House)

Words and Music by BRIAN DOERKSEN
and SANDRA GAGE

* *Recorded a half step higher.*

SING TO THE KING

Words and Music by
BILLY JAMES FOOTE

TO THE ENDS OF THE EARTH

Words and Music by MARTY SAMPSON
and JOEL HOUSTON

all the world __ will see __ that You are __ God, You are __ God. _____

TRADING MY SORROWS

Words and Music by
DARRELL EVANS

UNASHAMED LOVE

Words and Music by
LAMONT HIEBERT

WE LIFT YOU UP

Words and Music by
GLENN PACKIAM

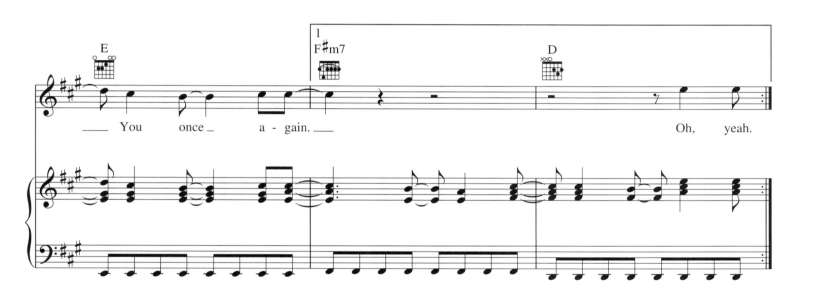

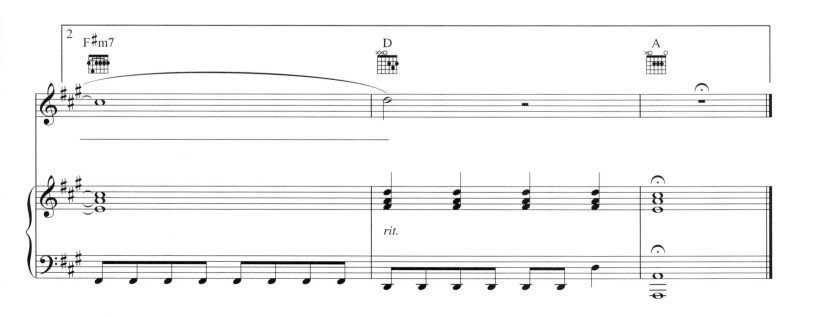

WE FALL DOWN

Words and Music by
CHRIS TOMLIN

YOU ARE GOOD

Words and Music by
ISRAEL HOUGHTON

and You are ___ good. ___

So good, so good, so

good.

YOU ARE HOLY
(Prince of Peace)

Words and Music by MARC IMBODEN
and TAMMI RHOTON

YOU ARE MY KING
(Amazing Love)

Words and Music by
BILLY JAMES FOOTE

You are ___ my ___ King.

You are ___ my ___ King. Je - sus, You are ___ my ___

___ King. Je - sus, You are ___ my ___ King.

D.S. al Coda
(with repeats)

CODA

Asus A G A D

In all ___ I ___ do, ___ I hon - or You. ___

YOUR NAME

Words and Music by PAUL BALOCHE
and GLENN PACKIAM

*Recorded a half step lower.

YOUR GRACE IS ENOUGH

Words and Music by
MATT MAHER

YOUR LOVE IS DEEP

Words and Music by DAN COLLINS,
SUSANNA BUSSEY KIRKSEY and JAMI SMITH

YOUR NAME IS HOLY

Words and Music by
BRIAN DOERKSEN

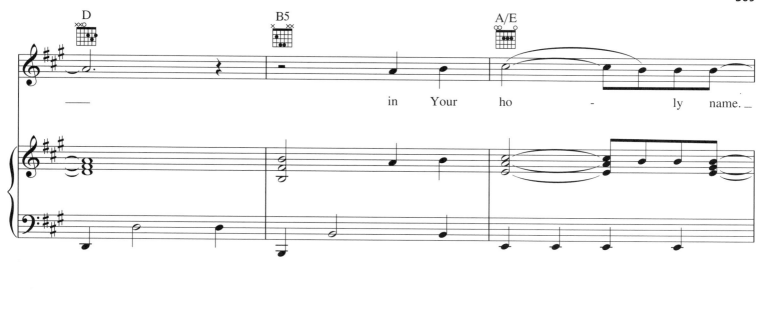

in Your ho - ly name. ___

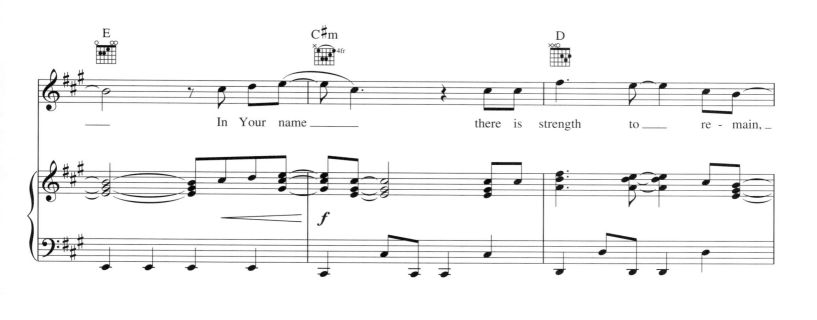

In Your name _____ there is strength to ___ re - main, __

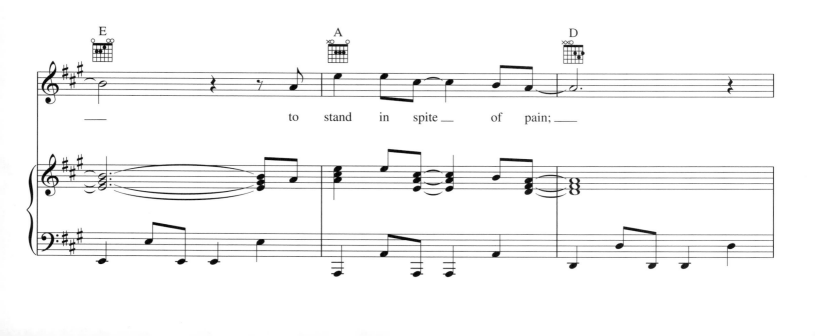

to stand in spite ___ of pain; ___

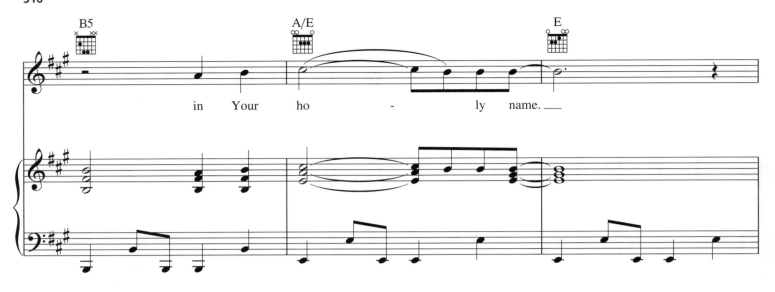

in Your ho - ly name. ___

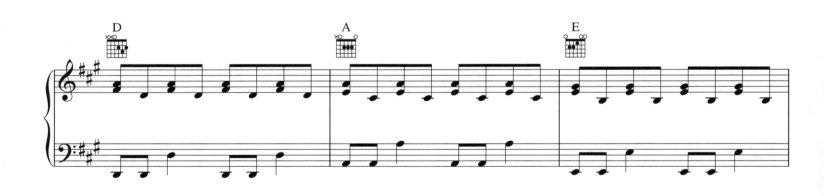

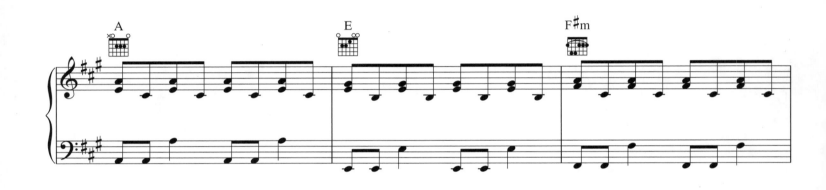

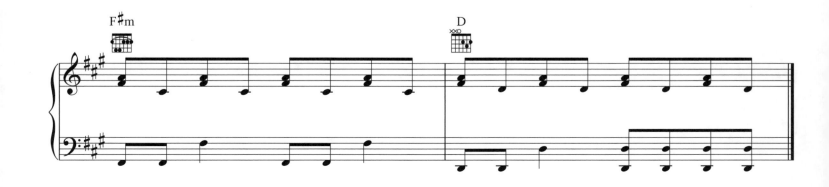